WINTER'S PROMISE

AND OTHER POEMS

Eric Palmieri

HIGH SERVICE BOOKS

NORTH PROVIDENCE, RHODE ISLAND

Property of High Service Books

Historic Fruit Hill
North Providence, Rhode Island 02911

Published by High Service Books

ISBN-13: 978-0692537374
ISBN-10: 0692537376

For Lily

CONTENTS

Love all those who hate
With the full depth of your heart,
For they need it most

WINTER'S PROMISE

AND OTHER POEMS

December

The days grow darker early now,
The sun hangs low
In the afternoon it brushes against the horizon
Like a stranger on a busy sidewalk looking down;
They are so close yet so far apart.

The nights illuminate a blackened sky,
House by house and tree by tree
We see the flickering flames of electricity,
Reflecting upon the midnight snow
That flutters down so gracefully.

And while we sleep a candle burns,
Not of day and not of night,
An Eternal flame that warms our hearts
No matter how much we've grown
Apart It holds us close.

A Night on Old Fruit Hill

The air so cold and frozen still,
And trees that break the wind,
The sound of floor boards creaking
In an old New England home,
Laying quietly under quilted warmth

I close my eyes,
Surrendering to winter's sleep,
Drifting out beyond the Heavens

A splash of lime tree memories,
A dash of Pop's plum pies,
Blossoms picked from
Boston cherries
And peaches pink like
Florida skies

So soon I'll wake to a grand new dawn
Born of love in a world of hate,
The snake that strikes at the hearts of men
So swiftly charmed he is by Light,
Cast upon a world of ice
It melts it all and forms the sea,
The one that rests in Galilee
Upon the waters blessed by night,
We'll walk together, just
You and me

But the air is cold and frozen still,
Outside the house on Old Fruit Hill,
By faith and faith alone I know,
That spring will come,
Life will bloom,
There is a season of
Birth renewed,
And as for now I'll wait and pray,
For the age of Love will come one day.

In The Eyes of The World

Winter winds whip upon my face
The tears of the past,
Frozen in time,
I am paralyzed,
Leaning on the loving arms of Friends.

Not strong enough to stand,
My crippled heart is
In Your hands,
Oh Lord,
Let my cry come unto thee.

Held up to the Heavens,
My crippled heart,
Is smitten,
Cradled by Everlasting Love,
I am at peace.

Like an owl of the desert,
I take flight amidst the darkness,
Forever searching,
For The Light I've seen,
In the eyes of the world.

Be kind to yourself
With every beat of your heart,
God is listening.

On County Street for Christmas Time

The smell of hot-fresh cinnamon buns
Moving across the kitchen,
I hear the ghosts of Christmas
Past, present, and future,
Sitting around a table maple,
Love soaked wood dressed up
For the season cold and dark
The light of candles dance.

We sit together in the round,
Some in chairs,
Some on the ground,
A cornucopia of gifts
Packaged with care,
Bursting out of our stockings
We share
In Divine abundance;
That's where
The joys of Christmas can be found.

Spirited songs we carol,
The midday sun shining
Through the parlor window,
A glimpse of spring we see,
The world reborn in fragrancy,
We celebrate the Birth of Life
Within,
Our hearts like Angels sing
An everlasting melody.

Holding hands In silence we give thanks,
For the candied scent of Christmas
Morning turns to night,
Aromatic spice and holiday fare
Upon our plates they fill the air,
Our bellies stuffed
With sweet delight
We bear witness to each other's light.

Standing at the door
We say goodbye
For now, we'll have our memories,
Always with us as they are,
The ones we love
We'll count among the many stars,
The night we shared the greatest gift
Of all our lives
On County Street for Christmas time.

Underneath The Christmas Tree

The electric rainbow fills his eyes,
Captivating and warm,
A mother reaching out
To her child
She offers memories
To a man grown
Up and away
From time gone by.

On hands and knees,
The soft brown carpet between
A child's fingers create a spark
Beneath the green plastic tree,
Imagination is warm milk
On a cold winter's night,
An old friend long forgotten
Appears within his blue-green eyes.

A carousel of colors
Slowly turning,
A kaleidoscope of possibility
Mesmerizingly seductive to a child's mind,
A palate of peppermint pops and gooey gumdrops,
Candy canes and Christmas trains,
Crystal ice and apple spice
A wonderland of winters past.

Here again,
Home again,
Walking up the slippery steps
I grab a hold of love
Never letting go
I'm safe and sound,
Where I want to be
Underneath the Christmas Tree.

Winter's Sleep

So cold it is
This time of year,
An Arctic chill descends
Upon my skin,
I feel the wind,
Teeth like broken glass
Beneath my feet
A mirror forms,
An icy sheet,
Atop a bed of rocks
A blanket gently falls,
White fleece
Like sparkling wine
Catching the light of dawn,
Before it's gone,
Bounces off
The blue spruce pines,
The small town streets they line,
All quiet now,
For winter's sleep
She's here,
She's here.

Each snowflake that falls,
Catching the Light of Heaven,
Sparkles forever.

Winter's Promise

February's freshly fallen
Snow atop a frozen pond,
A loosely knitted shawl
Draped across its shoulders,
Shivering quietly
The hardened skin of Winter
Softened
By the lightness of its form-

A world of white is born,
One so soon will slowly die,
Wooden soldiers standing by
With open eyes
They see the coming Spring,
Their naked arms outstretched,
Their bony fingers broken,
Laying lifeless on the ground-

A gently beating heart
The maple tree,
Sleeping soundly amidst
A blizzard's battering breath
Awaits the Southern sun,
To warm the veins
An awakening that lies in wait
All Winter long-

The silent song of Life reborn,
In days that yet to come
Give promise to a world
Cut up by cold stone walls,
Centuries old but not as strong.

The Village Dance

O how I love
The village dance,
A carousel of friendly faces
Comes alive
With simple graces;
We all join hands.

The frenzied fiddler catches fire,
The guitar player's plucking wires
A mandolin rains down love;
For The Lord above
We'll share good cheer
With all the ones we hold so dear.

Now hoots and hollers fill the air,
The men with fresh pressed collars
Wear their finest boots;
They hit the floor of native pine
While keeping time
With good ole country flair
The ladies twirl
Their fancy skirts
Cast flirting looks
Upon their partner's eyes
They see reflections of the past
In double time,
Now twice as fast,
The days of youth reborn.

But now it's time to say goodbye,
The midnight hour drawing nigh,
We share a lover's waltz,
Carried off by hearts aloft
We float across the wooden floor
Together;

Amidst our fellow Friends
Our Light shines through
And through our lives
We'll dance together
Step by step for evermore
Just me and you.

The Best Birthday Ever!

Well look at you
You silly old fool,
What'd you do
With the guy I knew?

I'd have to say
He's gone away,
And if I may
I'm here to stay

What's that you say?
No time to play?
That's no way
To grow old and grey

I got things to do,
Can't you see?
I've got no time
For pleasantries

There's calls to make
When ovens break
I can't even bake
For goodness sake!

Let's order in
We'll watch the Sox,
Just like the time
We had chicken pox!

Baseball eh?
It's on too late!
I'll be asleep
Before they reach the plate!

Let's leave it
For another day,
We can catch some rays
Down by the bay!

Where the watermelons grow?
No way, can't go,
The air in my tires
Is getting low!

Let's take our bikes,
We'll ride in style,
We haven't done that
In a real long while!

I wish I could,
It sounds like fun,
But I've got so many
Damned errands to run!

I got things to do
Can't you see?
I've got no time
For pleasantries

There's people to see
And places to go,
It's not up to me,
You just don't know!

But today is our birthday
For you and for me,
To play is my plea
So what will it be?

A day by the sea?
A game on TV?
Heck let's get some wine
And some crackers and brie!

Tell me your wish,
Whatever it be,
Let's make this birthday
A grand jubilee!

If there's one thing I wish,
For you and for me,
It's to spend more time
With our family

So pick up the phone!
Let's give them a ring!
We'll all get together,
We'll dance and we'll sing,
We'll take lots of pictures
So we won't forget,
The good times we had,
The table we set,

The food, O the food!
All the food we did eat!
So much in fact
We can't see our feet!
Thank you, O thank you,
I'm grateful my friend,
A note I will write,
A card I will send…

This was the best birthday ever…

THE END!

Violence is a weed—
Allowed to grow and prosper
Kills flowers of love.

Mourning Mist

There's a distant aching
In my heart,
The soft horror of far away
Cries echoing
In the deepest caverns,
A slow drip slices through
The silent howl of emptiness,
Rising to the surface
A soothing mist,
Broken,
A violent burst of desert heat
Cutting through
Its fragile skin,
Ripped apart by
Hate evaporates,
The last gasp of life
Carried aloft,
Into the Arms of Heaven,
Its tender cradle rocked
By the Hand of God

The Shadows

The light of the rising sun
Cast early morning shadows
Upon the buildings there,
A man sitting on a bench,
A child,
Running up and down the sidewalks,
Joyful,
Innocence in full bloom
While the birds of summer
Sing a happy tune,
A calm wind,
Carries the salted air of the pacific
Over the landscape like a mother
Holding her infant son against her breast.

An old woman stands
Alone,
In the shade of a ginkgo tree,
It's shadow too thrown upon the ground,
Giving shelter from the summer sun.

And In that moment came
A falling star,
Upon which one dares not wish,
An Earth-bound supernova.

Bringing death
Upon the masses,
An explosion of white heat
Traveling the speed of light,
Freezes time.

They're all gone now,
Turned to dust
Settling upon the smoldering ruins
Of a once great city.

Death lingered for a while,
Walking through
The fires of hell,
And not a soul remained,
But then,
Upon ashen sidewalks,
Upon the skeletons of
Hiroshima left
Standing in the wake of evil,
He found their shadows there,
Burned forever
Into all our eyes,
The living
Memories that will never die.

Let us be stewards—
Tending the gardens of Earth
With dirt on our hands.

The Sower

The Lord above waits not
For the song of Spring
To spring
Surprises of nature's nature
Upon the unsuspecting
Masses
Held in silent prayer,
The resurrection of Life
Not here nor there
But where
The seed of growth
Lay quiet
Still,
Beneath the frosted skin
Of Winter's death,
Within the heart
Of Mother's womb
We're born anew,
Who knew?
Who knew the cradle of Life
Was rocked
By the soiled hands of God?

Mother's Day

Faceless beauty like smoke
From a smoldering fire rises,
The Spirit of Life reborn
Out of heat and light,
Takes flight,
Soaring above the charred remains,
Of countless cedars turned to dust.

Ashes scattered across the plains
Their Mother rains down tears,
Rolling off Her glacial cheeks
They come to rest beneath Her feet,
The scorching coals on which She walks,
Cooled by sorrow,
Fueled by lust,
We must entrust our one tomorrow
To skies of blue,
Red roses too,
To see them bloom,
For me and you,
And make for ourselves,
Such a wonderful world.

In the darkest night
The Earth never stops spinning;
Dawn will always come

Heartland

The Heavens rain down tears;
Upon the salted Earth
The drops do fall,
Slow at first,
A gentle tapping on
Rural housetops
Lends an air of comfort
To a troubled land

The heavy beating of
A solemn heart
Softened by the sounds
Of nature's song;
The rhythm of the rain,
The winds on the plain,
The Great Horned Owl's call
It's all I hear

While crickets sing,
Their strings in chorus
Fill the prairie's concert halls
With nocturnes and lullabies

Hush
The cries of tired babes,
Laid to rest
With loving care.

From the tender cradle
Of a Mother's arms
They'll dream of
Tomorrow,
When Light and Love
Fill the Eastern sky,
Beyond the long horizon line
In the fires of the rising sun.

Lemon Tree

There is a lot of me I see
When watering this lemon tree,
The simple smell of citrus
Leaves
Once greenish hues
Begin to flee

Wilted ones
They hide behind new growth,
Curling up in fetal form
They shiver
At the sight of dawn

But O, this little lemon tree
In early Spring,
Branches out,
Stretching far
Beyond the blue

Not set in stone,
The Earth will turn,
Beneath the ground
The roots of Love and Light reside
Inside the bed we've made

O, lemon tree grow
Fruits of Life
Among the Winter shadow's night
By this I'll know It
On and on…

Light is Light alone without
A thing on which to shine upon

Darkness will become
A world of Eternal Light,
Born out of kindness

Mystic

The wind-blown waters of
Rocky shores
Crash with violent rage
Against the morning mist of
Autumn's dawn,
Rising above the mighty cliffs

A child's dream,
Clouds of colors bright
Are born that never die
While Father's hand
Lay intertwined
With mine

The grasses grinning
gently brush
Upon my cheek,
They tickle me,
The salted air of
Summer splashing
Savory sweet
Like taffy stuck between my teeth

I walk the sandy boardwalks,
Blue and grey
Beneath my feet
They lead
The way to Immortality.

Native Place

No more shall the clocks toll
   For the grounded man,
Dwelling down below
   The frozen ponds of New England,
Failing to grasp
   The airy notions of surface life.

The geese soaring above in tight formation
   Know the way to warmer places,
Only to return
   Upon the dawn of Spring,
Heavenly fowl
   Landing gracefully.

On the open fields,
   Their songs echo against the squawking gulls,
Hovering with perfect poise
   Above the wispy whitecaps formed by a Northeast wind,
Gently blowing
   The sand about the dunes of Ogunquit;

The native birds know their rightful place
   Whereas the traveling man
Knows not his home,
   Always searching
For flowers in Fall,
   Or the Winter's evening sun.

And all the while
   The great horned owls call
To the rising moon of a starry twilight,
   Here I am,
O Faithful Friend,
   Here I am.

The Gorges

Driving out beyond
The sands of broken time,
Everlasting truth,
Sketches of foreign lands
Matching the stories of long ago,
Free to be

The second wave of justice,
Feeling, loving,
Balancing the weight of the world

On my fingertips,
Great walls have fallen down
The bricks of blood and gore
Drowning under tired hands,
Washed in the river
Gorges carved by magic;

Youth will
Never die
As long as Father dreams

Tides and Tempests

Sleeping on a Sunday afternoon,
(Calm in the wake of a sudden storm),
Waves of Light recede from view,
Grains of sand awash in brine,
Like salted grist
In the wounds of time

The balmy breath of a mid-day zephyr,
(Hush now, child)
Wafting over dunes,
Through the local flora there,
Finds its way across my sill,
Fanning gently upon my hair

I awaken to the blast of thunder,
(Like trumpets blaring
From beyond the brilliant bluffs)
The foreboding gloom of somber skies
Can be seen for miles and miles,
Reflected in my waking eyes.

Early morning Light
Lifting the black veiled night
Married sun and moon.

A Quaker Baptism

Sitting in simple silence
The Spirit fills my heart,
The water of a raging river,
Ferocious,
Foaming at the mouth,
Comes crashing down with
A thunderous clap.

Churning up the sandy bottom
It finds peace in the Pool of Life,
Still,
A fire burns within,
The Light of Love
In ripples shine,
Formed by the mighty falls.

Now I hear the sounds serene,
A gently flowing stream,
(The sparkles
Of a thousand suns),
I'm born again,
In the Blessed waters
Of an Everlasting dream.

Lymansville

The summers were hotter
Back then,
Great big trees
Taller than the heights of freedom,
Morning air
Filled with the scent of gasoline
And fresh-cut grass,
Running out
Beyond the fences to an open field,
Playing ball,
The salty sweat on our foreheads
Biting at our freshly burned skin.

The sound of cicadas
Like high tension power lines
Over our heads,
The sun veiled by a misty haze,
The bluest sky turned
Plum red and tangerine.

The pavement is a hot plate
Under our feet,
The sands of winter
Sticking to our soles like cockleburs,
Washed off at the spigot
'Round back of the house.

The sound of a bug zapper
Frying mosquitos
Against a symphony of crickets,
The aroma of charred
Hamburg and pork sausage
Clinging to the brume that rises
From the grill like smoke signals,
And after supper we'd walk to Grandma's
For an evening swim,
The pool aglow,
As the brutal heat
Lingered In the night.

Sunday Dinners

Dinners on Sundays
Held at two or three o'clock,
Pasta forever

Three generations
Gathering in the kitchen
Memories are made

Dipping hard-crust bread
Into simmering gravy
When no one's looking

Garlic, O garlic,
Savory spice of my dreams,
I love you on bread

Voices loud and sharp,
Shoot across the tabletop,
We talk with our hands

Can someone say Grace?
Madonna mia, mangia!
Morta da fame!

Simple God

I saw God today,
Walking down the avenue,
Dressed in simple clothes.

Wearing simple shoes
The God of Life was skipping,
Singing simple tunes.

Heavenly smiles,
On all the children's faces,
Simply loving life,

By the Grace of God
I felt my love light shining,
Lighting up the world.

Dressed in simple clothes,
Walking down the avenue,
I saw God today

With God Inside

The quiet creak of the floor below
Filling the silent void
A child's bubbling laugh;
It's all I hear.

I find my place
For worship's sake
I close my eyes
Before I see the Light.

God's in front of me,
I breathe in love and out it comes,
Peace,
Full with Joy.

I pray to thee,
My God,
Is the beating of my heart
Keeping time in eternity?

Meeting the warm air around me,
I slowly dissolve,
In shape and form,
I am reborn

In Spirit,
I am alive in this world
With God inside,
I am.

Appeal to Heaven
When injustice rules the day,
Heal all wounds with Love.